LIFE ON MAR'S

A Four Season Garden

Mar Jennings

Mar Jennings and Corky Von Schnorkenheimer

Photography by Melissa Markris-Diluca

"From an empty landscape,
I created an intimate world
of abundant beauty that
I call home."

This book is dedicated to Edward R. Smith—mentor, devoted friend and confidant whose encouragement, patience and guidance helped me secure a solid foundation for my life and the courage to live my dreams. Your short but meaningful life touched all those who had the good fortune and pleasure to know you. You will forever remain in our hearts.

Acknowledgements

This book would not have been possible without the help and encouragement of many, particularly all the avid gardeners who generously participated in the garden tours which inspired me to "play in the dirt" and begin my own gardening journey.

My wonderful paternal grandmother gave me my first introduction to gardening and also my first watering can. She taught me about sharing plantings and giving the gift that keeps on giving.

My mother's love, devotion and sacrifice helped me become a competitive athlete. The dedication and discipline of that endeavor helped me tap into my inner strength, and gave me the courage to pursue my dreams.

My dear friend, Edward, introduced me to the world of roses. His instruction, direction and wisdom can forever be seen throughout my garden.

I am grateful to the many people of Westport and Fairfield County, CT who came to visit my home and gardens for numerous garden tours. Your words of encouragement and appreciation for my efforts have served to validate my mission.

SJ S&J Publishing, Westport, CT 06880
To order, visit us at www.marjennings.com

ISBN 978-1-60461-195-3

Contents

Introduction

Life on MAR'S: A Four Season Garden is a photographic essay documenting the four seasons of a Connecticut garden as seen and photographed through the eyes of garden master and lifestyle expert, Mar Jennings.

This remarkable garden journey takes you on a private walk through his Westport, Connecticut home, garden studio and gardens. Inspired by Mar's many visits to the English countryside and classic English gardens of London, the outdoor garden studio completes this enchanted ivy and vine dwelling. Using a seasonal approach, Mar leads you on a detailed tour beginning with the vibrant colors of summer.

This special photographic journey documents ten years of evolution, designing and refining, culminating in a splendid garden. Mar's yard unfurls perfectly in vivid images from spring through winter no matter where you look. Clever and creative is the overall response as Mar walks you through his in-town oasis. Architectural design elements and details abound in this small, but provocative garden. It intrigues the senses as each season approaches. Mar's garden awakens with interest no matter what time of year.

Mar's home and garden design concepts have been featured in and photographed for numerous national, regional and local publications. His gardens have been visited by thousands who continue to be amazed by the beautiful specimen trees, shrubs, and perennials. His unique style warrants a stop, a pause and a deep breath of reflection.

This amazing book is packed with ideas and wonderful design elements that will inspire you to create your own four season garden. Mar teaches gardeners to plant and care for their landscaping as a professional would, and shares the names of the products he uses to get the job done. This is a fresh approach to garden design that won't break your back or bank account. You'll walk away with a little piece of what "Life on Mar's" is like, filled with new ideas, energy and determination, and some delicious recipes that you can enjoy year round.

Take a private tour through Mar's world of gardening as if you were there with him. This book provides beautiful garden detail, design and implementation ideas that are easy enough for novices and interesting enough for seasoned gardeners. Mar's no-nonsense approach keeps it simple so that anyone can learn, enjoy, and enhance the many benefits of a gardening experience.

Mar's tagline, "and there you have it" says it all.

"Whether large or small, your garden should offer an element of surprise."

About Rosebrook Gardens

Rosebrook Gardens is a home first and foremost. The energy and soul of this house and property are palpable from the first moment one sets foot on the Belgian block apron of the driveway. Every step closer to the house brings visual wonderment in every direction. You don't want to miss any piece or detail of this oasis, so it is quite often difficult to know which way to proceed. Do I go straight up the walkway to the door, or do I venture into the side yard under the pergola to get a better look at the profusion of flowers grouped in wonderful containers and cascading over the arbors and trellises?

Once inside, one feels the same energy and harmony as one feels in the garden. Vibrant color and texture abound on every floor and in every room. Unique garden ornaments surprise you, cleverly situated atop and among beautiful yet unpretentious antique furniture. The effect is one of casual luxury and welcoming refinement. The abundant and diverse roses of Rosebrook Gardens are the essence of the story which you are about to discover on the following pages. It is my gift to you.

Something New is Something Old

This property is part of a subdivision that was created in 1921. While other homes were built at that time, this property remained vacant, containing only overgrown trees and shrubs. In 1995, R. B. Benson and Co. purchased the property and began building in 1996. I purchased the newly built home in June of 1997. Although R. B. Benson and Co. did a fine job building this house, I spent a great deal of time upgrading and re-designing the home for style and comfort. I wanted to "turn back time" as it were, to give the house the feeling of having been restored rather than the "oh, there's the new house on the block" feel. I did this by carefully listening to items that spoke to me (like the old shutters on the garden studio), many of which are not high on the priority list for most new home owners. I chose to replace items that were brand new and perfectly fine because I wanted to create a softer and more interesting look for my home. Within the first year, for example, I replaced the aluminum gutters with copper ones which now in fact, have a wonderfully aged, verdigris look.

My original garden design has evolved as I have grown and evolved. What is now known as the garden studio is an exact replica of the house, only much smaller. Its size is the maximum that could be built given the size of the property. I spend a great deal of time there while working in the garden.

Why the name Rosebrook Gardens? It's simple. There is a brook at the end of the street almost in my backyard, and I love roses. In fact, is there anyone who doesn't? Although I have many species of flowering plants, trees, etc. throughout my garden, roses predominate in parts of it because they are such a special and magnificent flower.

Sharing a Garden

When I purchased my home, I began to focus on the garden and interior design ambitions bubbling inside me. I unleashed my drive and passion on this newest project. In the first week, I managed to coordinate exterior house painting, tree removal, installation of an irrigation system and initial construction of a small garage which became my garden studio. Trees were removed and replaced with others which became the foundation for the overall garden design. All this would come to seem quite trivial compared with what was to arrive that first Saturday morning.

Expecting workmen and deliveries later in the morning, I was somewhat shocked when I heard a knock. As I peered through the side panels of the door, I saw a very attractive woman beautifully dressed with a very stylish hairdo. My new next-door neighbor, Barbara, was standing at my door with a beautiful apple pie. Still in my robe no less, I opened the door to one of the sincerest smiles that I had ever seen. I had no idea that this gracious "welcome to the neighborhood" gesture would develop into one of the most profound friendships of my life. As she made her way back down the walkway, I reflected on how many times I had moved and had never received such a genuine welcome. This simple but powerful gesture left me pondering the cliché "love thy neighbor." I had no idea that I would find my new best friend in her simple act of kindness.

Not much has changed since that first meeting. I know I can count on Barbara to hold my hand when I'm sad and to feed me when I'm hungry. She is honest (brutally sometimes) with me about my life and manages to help me keep my feet on the ground. We have shared many life experiences together; some happy and some sad, but none as difficult as the loss of our dear friend Edward, without whom, our rose gardens would not exist today.

This is the story of a deep and enduring friendship that grew out of a desire to be good neighbors and our shared side-garden. No fences, no stone walls, just a passion to create a beautiful space abutting both our properties. Our adjacent side yards would ultimately become a topic of numerous newspaper articles and garden tours. Our lives have been enriched by our garden and our friendship.

In many communities, neighbors are often isolated and may not be inclined to do neighborly things. Being a good neighbor requires one to practice the art of being "thoughtful," such as a simple hello and a small offering like a pie or a houseplant. With houses getting bigger and yards getting smaller, the proximity of neighbors makes civility and consideration ever so much more important.

I'm convinced that gardens make good neighbors. This is one concept I believe in, live by, and have proof that it works. As I mentioned earlier, my amazing relationship with my neighbor grew out of our love for our shared side garden. So much so, that in fact, I'm now totally responsible for the day-to-day, season-to-season maintenance of not only mine, but hers too. What is the trade off, you might ask? The trade off is that she gives unconditional love to my schnauzer when I'm not home and gives me a grilled cheese on demand (most of the time). Not bad for a single guy like me.

Our shared garden began when I offered my services to work in the part of her garden that was in close proximity to mine. During the first few years, every weekend from early spring to fall, we ventured out to many garden shops, nurseries and discount home and garden stores. We always selected plants that were currently in bloom. And, with no real plan, we created a garden that blooms throughout the season; purple, pink and white in the spring and copper, yellow and orange in the fall with tons of hydrangeas that we cut and share with the neighbors. Our friendship grew simultaneously with our gardens and we now have a wonderful shared garden that has no boundaries.

Each year, I often bring overgrown shrubs that need to be relocated to one of my neighbors as a gift. I offer to plant it but more often than not, they prefer to get involved and plant it themselves. Other neighbors have taken notice and have asked for my assistance. Today the street is filled with gardens and my old castaways have found new homes not far from whence they came. It's funny how something that once grew in my yard is now growing in a neighbor's garden, as if it were all meant to be somehow. I get to enjoy the beauty that comes not only from my own property, but from my neighbor's as well.

Mar At Home

To know me is to understand my particular style, which is "casual luxury." My home is not only a haven for me and Corky, but for my friends as well. Nothing gives me greater pleasure than to share my home and garden with others.

When I was no more than twelve years old, I stayed home from school one day claiming to be ill. While my parents were at work and with my grandmother in the kitchen, I took it upon myself to rearrange the living room furniture and accessories. When my mother arrived back home, she said to me, "I thought you were sick?" I replied, "I was sick. But after redecorating the living room, I feel much better."

My mission is simple. Creating a beautiful home or garden is within everyone's reach. Everyone's home can be an oasis and it's my desire to inspire you to learn how easy and fun this can be. I hope that this book does just that.

"Living well is possible on a limited budget...you just need to explore the resources."

Corky in the Garden

Over the years, I have come to learn a lot about Schnauzers. I quickly learned that they talk back. Perhaps the real translation of "Schnauzer" is "workaholic." It doesn't matter if the size is miniature, standard, or giant, if it's a Schnauzer, it's most likely looking for a job to do.

No diva princess, this working dog has not only captured the love and adoration of many, she is the subject of much conversation in the garden. She continually provides inspiration for show segments and featured articles. Corky fills her time with play dates, guest appearances and afternoon respites, all the while guarding our home. The fact is, a busy, happy and friendly dog makes the perfect pet companion. I often say to my single friends, "if you want to meet someone, borrow a dog and go out for a walk." Corky is quite popular and has many human friends that take her out and about for hours at a time. She always returns with stories of her adventures and how she met all kinds of wonderful new people.

Historically, the type of work for which Schnauzers were bred varied with the dog's size. The minis were originally highly-valued ratters and tireless watchdogs on farms in Germany. Today, they are mostly companion dogs, but some Schnauzers continue to work. This means "look out" to any UPS or mail carrier coming to the door. Corky, my 16 pound little girl, will acknowledge you and ask: Why are you here? Bark, Bark, Bark. Who sent you? Bark, Bark. Don't I look cute in my pink collar? Bark, Bark, Bark. Excuse me, Bark Bark. Do you have any treats for me? Bark, Bark, Bark, Bark. You get the picture.

Hours can pass as I experience the joys of my little dog discovering all that is new in the garden. After all, she is a working Schnauzer and there is lots of work to be done: chasing squirrels, letting birds know who is in charge, and overseeing the property as security director. All visitors must be sniffed and announced while naps are squeezed in between. Unless it is raining or freezing, Corky prefers to be on duty outside for the day's work ahead. This is an endless job for man's best friend. The job of pet owner is to provide quality of life and to act responsibly. Corky has enriched my life in ways too numerous to mention here. One last thought: as much as you love your dog, your dog loves you many times more, and in their own canine way, they live to joyfully serve and love you.

"Mar's mine. Take a number."

— Corky

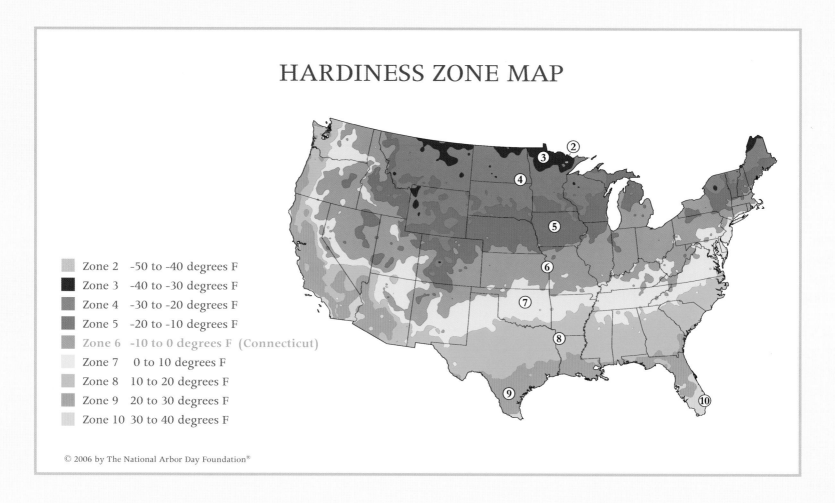

HARDINESS ZONE MAP

Zone 2   -50 to -40 degrees F
Zone 3   -40 to -30 degrees F
Zone 4   -30 to -20 degrees F
Zone 5   -20 to -10 degrees F
Zone 6   -10 to 0 degrees F (Connecticut)
Zone 7   0 to 10 degrees F
Zone 8   10 to 20 degrees F
Zone 9   20 to 30 degrees F
Zone 10 30 to 40 degrees F

Finding Your Zone

It is important to know which zone you are in when choosing plants for your garden. My home is located in Zone 6. Ask your local nursery professional which zone you are in if you don't know. Note that the first number in the range indicates the minimum temperature that plants can withstand in your zone. For example, Zone 6 indicates that my plants may be at risk when temperatures fall below -10 degrees, which it often does. A harsh winter can be devastating. When purchasing any plant, look for the appropriate zone for your area on the label. Whenever possible, it is advisable to purchase plants that can survive in one zone colder than your zone. This policy is often difficult to adhere to because when we see a new plant that we fall in love with, we often take the risk. Open, windy areas, raised beds and plants in winter-resistant containers where the root ball is above the ground can take a beating in winter. Through trial and error, you will notice winter kill occurring in specific parts of your yard. Protect the base of these exposed plants with hay or extra mulch. Many people in my zone put burlap over plants and bushes, but I never have and luckily, my winter kill has been minimal. Using evergreens as anchors throughout your garden can help to protect perennials from wind damage and harsh winter weather. Applying burlap is time consuming and back breaking work. For more information about any special conditions that may exist in your area, consult your local nursery professional.

"Attention to detail has become my trademark. Only when details are added to the garden will the harmony and style take shape. It is in the details that you create beauty and serenity."

Mar's Attention to Detail

Paying close attention to the details has always been my expertise and has become one of my most valuable trademarks. Here are my own professional recommendations about the d-e-t-a-i-l-s that will help you stay motivated, focused and on track.

D—Discover opportunities to create and enhance.

E—Evaluate the project.

T—Take the time to determine what's good and what is not.

A—Ask the professionals lots of questions.

I—Identify the things you will need.

L—Learn from your resources.

S—Start with a plan and timeline to help you finish.

The Roses of Rosebrook Gardens

No English garden would be complete without roses. Rosebrook Gardens is filled with them. Roses can be the most dramatic and spectacular plants in your garden. Putting time and energy into your roses will increase the number of blooms, prevent diseases and fungus, and improve the beauty of the display. For gardeners with little time, however, the time required to care for roses can be daunting.

No matter how hassle-free a rose is supposed to be, it must first have a beautiful fragrance. I never sacrifice this in a rose. In June, as the first massive flowering occurs, I delight in the exquisite rose perfume wafting through my garden. Here are a few of my favorite hassle free roses that will give you the total rose experience: fragrance and beauty.

By all means, cut your roses and bring them into the house. I like to entertain a lot in June and fill my house with rose bouquets from my garden. Guests arrive and often gasp at the picture-book beauty of a rose display on the mantle or on the dining room table. Plants continue to bloom right up until late October or early November. I place a small bouquet in every bathroom and on every bedroom nightstand for the sweetest garden dreams ever.

The specific things I look for in choosing a rose:

- **Climber, shrub or topiary (standard)**
- **Color**
- **Fragrance**
- **Size**
- **Disease and cold resistance**
- **Constant blooming throughout the season**

Mar's tips for growing MAR-velous roses

Ordering

Order bare-root roses in the fall for delivery in the spring. The internet is full of rose catalogues and suppliers.

Planting

Your soil should be humus rich and slightly acidic with a pH around 6.5. Choose a location that receives at least 5 hours of sunlight a day. Plant 18" apart if you are planting in groups or clumps. Plant among other perennials with an eye toward matching size and color. Plant your bare-root rose as soon as it arrives, preferably soaking it in water overnight. Dig a hole deep enough for the bud union to be about 4" below ground level. Add peat or manure (from the nursery) to amend the soil you have dug out and refill the hole with the rose in it. Mound the base with mulch, soil or compost until the plant leafs out.

Fertilizing

Fertilize regularly throughout the spring and summer. At the start of winter, heap mulch or hay around the plant to protect it until early spring.

Watering

Watering is essential, especially for new plants. Water roses at the root base with a slow trickle from the hose for 30 to 60 minutes per week. An in-ground drip line can be set to do this automatically. Roses like well-drained soil. Always mulch to keep the soil moist and weed free. If your rose dies mysteriously, it may well be poor drainage and/or not enough sun.

Brown Spots and Mold

Here is a recipe to help prevent your roses from getting brown spots and mold.

Equal parts skim milk and water. Put in a spray bottle. Spray liberally on the green, leafy parts of the plant. To achieve the best results, apply in the morning.

Pruning

Experts differ on when to prune. If a severe winter is on the way, a drastic pruning in the fall can weaken the plant. I always clean up the bush in late fall by simply cutting any long and unsightly canes with an eye toward maintaining the shrub shape that I want. Then, in early spring, before any buds or leaves appear, I cut out dead canes, shape the shrub and cut it down some, and clean up the interior of the rose bush by taking out the small criss-crossing canes and leaving the hardy, healthy ones with plenty of air between them. Roses love to be pruned because it stimulates the plant to send out plenty of fresh green canes in spring.

Cutting off dead blooms is called deadheading. Deadheading helps to increase the re-blooming of all roses. The more you deadhead, the more blooms you will have along with a neater looking plant. Cut the flower head off at about $\frac{1}{4}$" above the next 5-leaf joint on the same stem. Use sharp shears for a clean cut. Although most hardy roses will do relatively well without deadheading, the results will be much less spectacular.

"Rosebrook Gardens represents my love for my roses, my home and the special people who have touched my life."

	KIND OF ROSE	COLOR OF ROSE
UPRIGHT BUSH	Tamora	● Apricot
	William Shakespeare 2000	● Red
	Heritage	● Pink
	Molineux	● Yellow
	Graham Thomas	● Yellow
	Little White Pet	○ White
	Cameo Perfume	● Pink
	Queen Elizabeth	● Pink
CLIMBERS	Sombreuil	○ White
	Eden	● Pink, hints of yellow
	The Pilgrim	● Yellow
	America	● Salmon
	Climbing Iceberg	○ White
	New Dawn	● Pink
	White New Dawn	○ White
	Golden Showers	● Yellow
	Climbing Cecil Brunner	● Pink
	Colette	● Pink
	Blaze Improved	● Red
SHRUB / HEDGE ROSES	Carefree Beauty	● Pink
	Prairie Star	○ White
	Darlow's Enigma	○ White (Shade Tolerant)
	Bonica	● Pink
	Scarlet Meidiland	● Scarlet
FLORIBUNDA	Sunsprite	● Yellow
	Saratoga	○ White
GROUNDCOVER ROSES	Seafoam	○ White
	White Meidiland	● Pink

The Upside of Living Outside

If you're wondering if a beautiful garden is worth all the work and attention, I have to offer a resounding yes. Even though I frequently offer my garden for charity events and use it as the backdrop for MAR TV, it is the quiet moments that I spend in my garden that make it most worthwhile. I sometimes imagine that people think my garden is simply a stage for garden parties, teas and lunches for the "ladies who lunch" crowd. And while I have been known to "loan" my garden for a bridal shower or special celebration cocktail party, I love to entertain myself simply sitting in my own garden enjoying its beauty. This is my reward for the passionate attention I bestow on my garden. My inner child loves to play in the dirt, and I find strength in the peace and calm that comes with getting close to nature.

Like many people, I love to spend as much time outside as possible. I can be found in my garden at all hours of the day, on any given day, in any season. That said, I particularly cherish my mornings when I can relax and read the paper, sipping a cup of coffee in close proximity to and in full view of my garden. What a joy it is in spring, summer, and even warm fall mornings. You start to notice subtle differences in your plantings and the way the light changes the look and feel each day.

A new appreciation of nature starts to develop inside you, and soon you find yourself looking for all that is new. Corky is never too far away, surveying her domain as she scours the property to make sure everything is in order and looks for other furry, four-legged creatures that may be lurking about. Those of you with pets, particularly dogs, will understand how attentive they are to every sound and rustle, hoping for a whiff of a new exciting smell. Guests are always greeted by Corky first, as she is better than any doorbell, barking to inform me that I have a visitor.

And while I cherish the quiet most mornings, I do enjoy entertaining weeknights and on the weekends. Brunch is one of my favorite ways to entertain friends, one or two at a time. Sitting in the garden enjoying a light meal with a mimosa or two, relaxing, is a great way to enjoy the weekend, and catch up with someone you haven't seen for a while without the distractions that often accompany eating in a restaurant. And if you're single like me, a brunch in the garden can be the perfect setting for a romantic date.

A garden patio, terrace or deck provides the backdrop for any number of entertaining options. Afternoon garden parties, cocktails and intimate dinners are my favorite. Large parties can be overwhelming and often require recovery time. I find that having one or two friends or one couple over is such a nice way to repay an invitation without lots of planning and expense. When you entertain in small groups, it lets your friends know that you value spending quality time with them.

"Ladies walking in high heels in the garden offer a fabulous aeration opportunity."

And what should happen if it rains? Not a problem. With a small group, it's easy to transfer the party indoors. Just make sure that your dining table is free of clutter and ready to be used. And no matter what the time of day, a candle or two always makes the event more festive. I've been known to bring a candelabra outside to add drama to the table. Nothing is more beautiful than candlelight in the garden. It's simply magical. Ladies and gentlemen, husbands and wives, create a special date with your loved one by dining al fresco and making it special. Breakfast, lunch or dinner, it doesn't matter. Tuesday or Friday, it doesn't matter. And it doesn't matter if you prepare the food yourself or pick it up on the way home. The presentation and ambiance are what matters most. Take time to transfer the food to the "good" china that never gets used. Why not do it up right for that special someone?

Sometimes enjoying the great outdoors doesn't even require a meal to be special. When was the last time you made homemade lemonade? Were read to? Or you read to someone? Sounds funny doesn't it? But imagine yourself lying on a chaise under a shade tree sipping some yummy lemonade and just listening to the sounds of the birds or the voice of your partner reading you your favorite poet or writer. Magazines of the grocery store variety can be fun too because of their less serious nature. Keeping it light has its virtues sometimes. Just being able to sit back and listen is such a gift and so relaxing. Close your eyes and allow your mind to concentrate on what you are hearing. Stimulating conversation may ensue and then who knows what might happen! Perhaps some romance will spark? Stranger things have been known to happen!

Having a hammock available is a wonderful addition to a garden patio or yard. There is no better place for a lazy afternoon nap than under a shade tree. A picnic table under a shade tree is a wonderful place for doing arts and crafts with the kids or making fabulous flower arrangements. Bringing paperwork or your computer outside will make the chore go faster. Personally, I enjoy writing in my garden. The sights, smells and sounds of the garden fill the senses and bring a sense of well-being. And the fresh air will do you good after being inside all week.

Another way to enjoy being outside is to do chores outside. Does anyone wash their own car anymore? How about a family car wash? Kids love this, as it gives them a chance to play with the garden hose and get wet. You'll feel like a kid too while giving your kids the opportunity to learn responsibility and feel that they are contributing. They also learn that chores can be fun and enjoyable when done together. Planting and growing flowers and herbs with children is a wonderful way to get them interested in nature and let them experience the cycle of life and the miracle that is Mother Nature. It is one of the most wonderful gifts you can give them. Growing herbs with children is also a great way to get them interested in food that is healthy and delicious.

Spending time outside pruning and "deadheading" is a great way to get to know your shrubs and give them some much needed love and attention. Working outside in early morning or after work is a good way to clear your head before a stressful day or after one. The garden provides the perfect backdrop to connect with nature, de-stress and "smell the flowers," as it were. Some may choose to wear a digital music device, but I prefer to pay full attention to the job at hand and let the sights and smells consume me. Time flies by, the job gets done and I'm relaxed, maybe a little dirty and sweaty, but all the better for it! I've been told that this is a great look for me. All kidding aside, while I embrace the sentiment, you may not want to give me a hug!

A garden can provide many opportunities to get close to nature and your friends. And don't think a garden has to be a yard. There is no outdoor space that is too small for a little garden in my opinion. A small terrace or deck is the perfect place to grow potted herbs and flowers that might perhaps peak your interest and desire for more. I started my garden with containers and have continued adding, eventually building my little oasis. Whether you start with a small terrace or container, consider it a place to explore the endless opportunities that outdoor living has to offer. Before you know it, you will find that there are only upsides to living outside.

"Never bother or fret about the inevitable little grass stain. It's green. It's good. It works for me."

"*Life on Mar's is elegantly simple…and simply elegant.*"

The Garden Studio

I always dreamed of having a unique potting shed where I could spend hours playing in the dirt with a roof over my head. While researching potting sheds, I discovered that they were first introduced in Germany in the 1600s but did not become widely popular until the 19th century. These sheds usually had several windows and contained worktables of various sizes and all the tools and items necessary for gardening. But I wanted something different. I wanted something that was both functional and beautiful.

I created a potting shed for myself, although I call mine a "garden studio." At the 2004 Westport Historical Society Hidden Garden Tour, I was asked hundreds of questions about my garden studio. Later I was told that my studio was the hit of the tour! Converted from a former one-car garage, this space has been my newest gardening project and I use it throughout the year. It is my oasis when I need to escape from the world. Although not heated, it is well insulated and I keep a portable heater there in the winter just in case it gets really cold.

As I mentioned previously, the exterior of this structure contains many of the same architectural and design elements as the exterior of my home. I live by the adage that something old can become something new, and I'm always seeking out old things and finding new uses for them. My grandmother's old kitchen cabinet, rescued from the trash, stores books and fertilizers. Other design features include a Dutch door, floor-to-ceiling shelves, and a center island where I can arrange flowers and repot annuals I get from the nursery. The garage's once bare cement floor is painted in a black and white checkerboard pattern. It creates interest and makes the studio feel larger. More windows were installed, including a beautiful old window that I rescued from an old house that was condemned and about to be demolished. A plain garage door was soon replaced with a charming carriage door.

Whether you choose a simple structure or something more elaborate, a potting shed gives us grown-ups a place to escape from reality, an opportunity to get close to nature and a chance to play in the dirt. Here, one can find peace, beauty, and a sense of purpose. Your garden becomes a place of discovery, each season bringing with it new knowledge and experience that only nature can teach us.

"Garden ornaments are like punctuation in a novel.
They instruct you to pause and reflect."

The Four Season Garden

For over twenty-five years, I have been inspired to create and make things beautiful. However, creating a pleasant home and garden environment doesn't happen overnight. What you see on the following pages is what I have created over the past ten years. Each project has been an opportunity to learn, to understand the vast array of different home and garden styles, and has helped me fine-tune my own personal style for home and garden. I hope you will be inspired to embrace the opportunities and joy of gardening and design.

Transformation starts with a vision and a passion to change the way we look at things. Many times by simply repeating a basic design or geometric shape, you can create pleasant new surroundings. Textures and colors are your foundation. In the garden, base your selection of plants on the appropriate zone and the amount of light and shade that they will receive.

You can transform your garden with planning and dedication to understanding your space. No project is too small or too large. Start in one area and build year by year. Constantly asking questions will help you enjoy the time you spend creating your garden.

Summer Tour

With the pruning and planting of spring long done, the summer garden seems to just appear out of nowhere. The garden abounds with flowers and attracts the little animals in: the birds, the bees, the bunnies and the turtles. What a gift from Mother Nature! The hot and steamy hours of midday are not for gardening however, as I prefer to work early in the morning and in the evening when the heat has broken. With no one watching, my garden seems to effortlessly take care of herself.

Sitting under a shade tree or under the pergola, there is no shortage of things to delight the senses; the perfume of different flowers, the cacophony of sounds of different animals and the color and texture of the flora. Summer is here. This tour will offer more glimpses of Rosebrook Gardens. I hope you enjoy this journey through my eyes.

The entrance to any home should be welcoming.
Boxwoods line the entrance; stone dogs
(made in England) wait to greet you.
Last year, I added the lintel over the door to create
additional depth. In the fall, I place small pumpkins
on the lintel for visual interest. In the winter,
I drape evergreen garlands there.

A soft arch and picket fence separate the side yard from the front. Sombreuil roses burst up and over the arch in spring with pure white fragrant flowers. The gate opens, inviting visitors in to explore and discover, while creating a barrier through which one must pass to enter the "garden room."

Allium interspersed dramatically among the peonies pop early and last longer than the iris. Boxwood along the house guarantees color and texture year round.

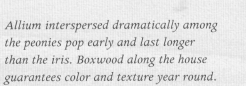

Two sections of a picket fence have large 6"x 6" pressure-treated posts. The posts are capped with a dentil molding to create a barrier to the street. Climbing clematis enjoys weaving itself among the pickets and boxwood below.

The magnolia tree or as I like to refer to it — MAR-nolia, presents an outstanding summer flower display. These lush, healthy leaves provide many creative projects for my home and garden. It's a Mar must have!

"Doggy see, doggy do, it's up to you to scoop the poo."

Left border of the property is lined with 24 emerald arborvitae, forming a privacy hedge. Beds on either side of the side-yard alleyway are lined with serpentine dwarf English boxwood hedges that mirror each other. Moss has grown on the bricks that were added to line the garden beds along the walkway and to direct attention towards the back garden. The bricks are half buried diagonally.

Plants can help soften homes, serving to better integrate them into the landscape. In this photo, White New Dawn and New Dawn roses intertwine with the clematis which covers and softens the exterior of the fireplace. A lilac topiary was planted for height and fragrance, and to momentarily draw the eye upward.

Lupine, allium and clematis grow with delight under the wall trellis which boasts New Dawn and White New Dawn climbing roses. This excellent color and texture combination create a garden vignette within the larger bed.

The back door landing was designed and created for morning coffee and easy access to the garden. An old cement planter complements this space with an annual Scaevola aemula. A time capsule was placed into the patio landing prior to its being filled with cement that tells the story of the garden and its homeowner.

Honeysuckle covers the side of the garden studio, focusing attention on the lion fountain. The sound of tinkling water delights those entering the studio and the backyard. Although workable, the early 20th century shutters were added for aesthetic detail, not function. I always endeavor to combine something old with something new.

Painted cedar window boxes add interest and style to any home. I love to plant dwarf boxwood with bacopa to fill in the gaps.
This provides color from April to November and winter interest as well. Copper gutters were added for lasting function and visual appeal.
A homemade armillary was added to create depth and interest to this small garden bed.

*"The garden studio...
the only thing missing
is a daybed!"*

Statues are an excellent way to create
a focal point on which to pause and reflect.
This little Pan statue was a real find at
a consignment shop in Westport.
Winter, spring, summer and fall, this little
man surveys his domain.

The garden studio, a former one-car garage, has gone through many transformations. Shelves line the back wall of the studio and hold a vast array of terra cotta pots. The island was a find on sale and is the perfect size for transplanting, arranging flowers and wrapping gifts.

Fragrant peonies clamber about a tuteur covered with honeysuckle serotina.

"Playing in the dirt, I love this job."

Over 200 dwarf English boxwoods line the back garden beds to create style and draw the eye along the undulating border.
No straight lines, just magnificent curves planned to enhance the visual appeal and create a sense of flow and softness.

Under the pergola, this former driveway is transformed into an intimate spot where one can retreat and enjoy a view of the side garden. The asphalt was replaced with Connecticut native crushed stone and provides a soft underfooting that is more durable than grass and more attractive than asphalt with less maintenance.

Deborah Herbertson introduces me during a charity luncheon and garden tour for the Westport Historical Society.

Birds add sound, wonderment and whimsy to a garden. This late 20th century birdbath sits close to a birdhouse. A lava ball was placed in the center to add interest and charm. Moss has now covered the lava rock and created a wonderful contrast to the lavender Baptisia and sage color.

Something old with something new works especially well when it is a bargain! This little distressed side table was a find at a local tag sale for twenty dollars. The once green table is perfect for this space, offering function and style. Two cedar chairs with down pillows invite you to sit and relax.

Hydrangeas are one of my favorite flowers and I have many varieties. Its splendid flowers are the gift that keeps on giving. The Macrophylla hydrangea ranges from shades of blue to pink, depending on soil pH, and continue to bloom way into the fall providing months and months of flowers. After November, I put clippings of rose-purple Peegee hydrangea in window boxes for fall and winter enjoyment. Along with evergreen clippings, this adds interest to any window box when most blooms in the garden have begun to wane.

No matter what time of year, the English boxwood always packs a bold emerald green punch of color and texture. Small, dense leaves maintain a colorful lushness year-round. I mix boxwood with white impatiens for contrast. Ivy softens the look of an unattractive cement foundation wall and adds color and texture. Maintenance and continual cutting are important to keep the ivy from getting out of control and climbing up the wood siding of your house.

Roses given to me as a hostess gift are mixed with sedum from my garden. The roses and sedum are packed tight and tied with a rubber band before the stems are cut short for this silver goblet.

Rose bouquets are both fragrant and be
The abundant blooms seem never-end

The Peegee hydrangea in topiary tree form is a fanciful addition to any garden. Each year in the fall, I cut off all the blooms in order to maintain the original topiary shape. By fall, the flowers are vibrant in color and size. I create large arrangements for the house and still have dozens of blooms to give to friends and neighbors.

A Drink of Water

For most gardeners and particularly serious ones, the most time consuming and difficult task is watering. Many people use the traditional method of standing in the garden with a hose and enjoy the time spent watering the garden. Some of us, however, are looking for maximum rewards with minimal work. I love and depend on an irrigation system. If financially accessible, I strongly suggest that gardeners protect their investment with an irrigation system that covers the lawn as well as all the garden beds with a combination of drip lines and sprinkler heads. Roses, for example, flourish with a drip system as opposed to direct watering.

The lushness of a late August garden and a verdant lawn are usually signs that the plants and lawn are being watered daily. My own lawn stands out in brilliant green in late summer.

Before investing in such a system, do your homework: find at least three sprinkler contractors, and get quotes plus a plan of where the lines and watering heads will be placed. Remember the price usually depends on the square footage and number of heads, so ask questions and see if the number of heads can be kept to a minimum—just enough to reach everywhere, but not overlapping. You can always add more at a later date for new and expanded garden beds. I recommend that you be present when the system is installed and check the height of the heads and be sure the water reaches all your plants. Drip lines work best around roses, trees and evergreens. Keep your roses free from mist or direct watering to prevent diseases.

Your contractor should give you guidelines for watering times. Newly-seeded lawns have special requirements. Lawns in general may need different watering times and frequencies than your perennial beds.

My irrigation system gives me the time and energy to concentrate on planting, mulching, transplanting, pruning and enjoying my garden instead of constantly watering it. Sometimes I turn on the systems so the neighbors' kids can watch and enjoy the waterworks display. Irrigation systems help you protect your investment. If you are spending the money on landscaping, include an irrigation system in the budget. This technology will make gardening easier and more fun.

I always enjoy having a great salad with my meal. I created this simple salad for that perfect light addition to any meal.

This is an ideal refreshingly delicious salad for spring and summer. You can make a small amount for one meal, or make a couple of pounds and eat it all week long. In the summer, go to your local farmers' market for fresh tomatoes, basil, onions and cucumbers.

Summer Salad

- Kosher or sea salt & fresh pepper
- Ripe tomatoes (cut into 1"chunks)
- ½ red onion, thinly sliced
- 10-15 large basil leaves chiffonade*
- 1-2 kirby cucumbers, peeled and thinly sliced
- Small 1"cubes of fresh mozzarella cheese
- Good extra virgin olive oil to taste

*Chiffonade: I had to learn what this word means too. Stack 10-15 large basil leaves one on top of another. Roll into a tight cylinder. Slice small strips. They look like little green ribbons.

1. Cut up ingredients, mix in a large bowl, add olive oil and a splash of balsamic or red vinegar (optional), salt and pepper. Adjust the quantities of each ingredient by eye as you go along. I love cucumbers, so I always put in lots of those. Leave on the counter and serve at room temperature.

2. Fill plastic containers with individual servings and take them to the beach or on a picnic.

The Bumble Bee Summer Cocktail

- 1 pitcher, half filled with ice
- 1 bottle of French style lemonade (assorted varieties available. I prefer pink.)
- 1/2 bottle of sparkling water (I prefer S.Pellegrino®.)
- 1 lemon or lime, sliced into thin rounds
- 1 cup vodka (This amount may be adjusted to your own personal taste.)

As summer heats up, we begin to spend more time outside with family and friends enjoying the wonderful weather. Here is an incredibly easy summer drink I created with my friend, "Miss Bee," to help cool down from those hot summer days.

Perfect for any occasion, this delicious "Bumble Bee" cocktail will have you coming back for more. Serves up to six people.

1 Fill the pitcher with ice. Add the vodka, lemonade, S.Pellegrino®, lemons and/or limes. Stir and serve over ice. It doesn't get any easier than this!

2 A little vodka (one cup) offers a lovely "buzz." But "bee" careful, a little too much, and you just might get "stung!"

Whatever you choose…this is a tasty summer drink that will keep you cool, refreshed and relaxed.

Fall Tour

As summer's end draws near, I look into my garden and mentally prepare for the transformation that will soon take place. Autumn is just around the corner and this means an end to the garden parties that I love so much. But with some of the most brilliant colors yet to be displayed, I can enjoy my garden's last blooms. From years of observation, I have planned for each season, carefully selecting plants and shrubs that will complement each other both visually and functionally. I can relax and experience the change with nary a tool in sight.

A lava ball, simply placed on a birdbath, offers a resting place for its visitors as well as the perfect place for moss to grow. An example of beauty and function.

I will do with

My garden studio is a working room
where I also enjoy the fruits of my labor.
Hydrangeas are never in short supply.
I take advantage of their beauty by keeping
a large arrangement where I'm working.

"All you can carry for a quarter" said the sign at a local garage sale. I returned home,
picked up a bucket and loaded up. What a find! I placed the bucket along my gravel
driveway and left them to weather. I'm not quite sure what I will do with all these
small terra cotta pots, but I'm sure it will be something creative and fun.

The Peegee hydrangea is one of my most favorites. The mop-head flowers provide an endless supply of blooms that make wonderful dried flowers. Every garden should have one or maybe even two.

Adirondack chairs don't normally come in black unless I get my hands on them. Everyone scoffed at the idea. So, one Saturday afternoon I decided to listen to my gut and I painted them a high gloss black. This easy afternoon project transformed my common, everyday Adirondack chairs. As for my friends, well, "I told you."

When people tell me they have a black thumb, that they kill everything, I recommend succulents. The sedum will endure more than a few missed waterings and can survive in the most neglected gardens. Neglect is nothing compared to the harsh conditions that succulents endure in their homelands. A bumble bee has landed to enjoy the flowers of this hardy and beautiful shrub.

The Silver Lace trumpet vine is an aggressive vine that requires pruning each year. Trim late in the winter for a spectacular display in the fall. Here the soft, delicate white flowers cover the back garden fence against a lush green backdrop.

"Take charge of your garden. Mother Nature is watching."

Window boxes should always look great no matter what the season. Here I transformed the look into fall by adding dried hydrangeas, magnolia leaves and hemlock clippings. When placed in this type of arrangement, they provide a fabulous display of texture and interest whether viewed from indoors or out.

The combination of Myrtle and Creeping Jenny are wonderful under the River birch tree. For years, I struggled to perfect this area. Now I'm delighted with results that require no maintenance.

The Montauk daisy is a wonderful alternative to the average fall mum. Two galvanized buckets are used for planters rather than terra cotta pots. Guests are welcomed with something interesting and surprising.

The Tar Diva hydrangea is yet another white flower that adds interest to my hydrangea collection. Its long-lasting blooms can be dried and added to flower boxes or urns.

A peek through the window of the garden studio provides a glimpse of some of the hydrangeas that are now in abundance in the studio. The studio provides a bright, warm, covered space in which to dry all the hydrangeas that I choose. (Trust me, it's excessive!)

"Make any changes to the garden now. Old Man Winter will soon arrive."

The Butterfly bush grows a flower that is very inviting to butterflies. Although supposedly hearty enough for zone 6, the last three winters have not been kind to my Butterfly bushes. Regardless, each spring I continue to replace them because the flowers are well worth the effort.

Through careful training, an espalier creates a tiered, "two-dimensional" tree. This dramatic gardening technique, requiring years of care and patience, begins with a single radical step, as seen here with my Fuji apple. Fuji apples have it all. They're super sweet, super juicy and super crisp. What a great snacking apple! The Fuji's appearance varies from yellow-green with red highlights to mostly red. The Fuji's spicy, crisp sweetness gives it exceptional eating quality.

The herb garden takes a break in the late fall but still provides an interesting view of the side garden. This is a perfect place to read and enjoy a quiet, warm autumn day.

The "art of the birdhouse" is evident in my garden. With all the beauty that Mother Nature offers, I like to provide housing for our feathered friends. Good for the birds and great for the garden.

"After the lazy days of summer, the first crisp, fresh air of fall reminds me that soon I'll be putting my garden to rest."

Bacopa is an annual that continues to bloom right up to the first frost. Bittersweet, an aggressive vine that was taken from the woods, adds a punch of color to the already lush green Alberta spruce topiary.

A beautiful front yard view through the side gate provides a clear display of autumn arriving. In all seasons, Rosebrook Gardens provides an endless amount of beauty to discover and ponder.

The final work to be done is the fall clean-up, scheduled within the next two weeks. The garden is at rest and so am I. Soon, winter will arrive with its own special beauty.

The last of the Clematis Evithree are pushing up to bloom against all odds, indicating that our first frost is near.

I discover the versatility of ornamental grasses in my garden year-round. The combination of grasses with other garden plants provides for both subtle and explosive color effects. I love using grasses to bring exquisite textural components to each season.

A driveway can be both great looking and functional when an apron of Belgian blocks are added at the street end. Cement and stone dust secure each block in place. The look is more natural, softer and offers an easier transition to your yard, house or garden than an unnatural, black asphalt driveway.

The Giving of Trees

As a gardener, I thrive on the joy of personal achievement through the beauty of my garden and on giving back to those who enjoy the pleasures of life in the garden. By tending my garden, I make contact with the elements of life as I fine tune my skills and look to expand the ideas I have created. Gardens are metaphors for life and death. Flowers, for example, are forever changing. They come and go — some to return year after year and others only for the current season. Life and the parallel universe we share with our gardens mean even more to me when referring to trees. So often, many of us take for granted the trees that surround us. Do we take the time to really enjoy what they have to offer? As we enter autumn, who cannot notice the beauty and vibrant colors that we love here in New England? The amazing colors represent the change from season to season, just as we change and grow in our own lives. Trees are not just a part of the landscape of the communities we live in. They are very much alive and living among us. They feel pain, may become ill and sometimes even die. Trees enrich our everyday lives and offer us valuable lessons if we pay attention. They only ask for love and attention to survive.

My love for trees began as a child after reading the wonderful children's book, *The Giving Tree* by Shel Silverstein. I have cherished this book from the moment I read it, and today I continue to find new meaning in the simple lessons it teaches. This tender story, while touched with sadness, is aglow with consolation. Trees, it teaches us, not only provide the wood we need to build our homes, shade on a hot summer's day, but show us the gift of giving love, and a serene acceptance of another's capacity to return that love.

Planting a tree in celebration of a life or life event is something I learned many years ago from Jewish friends who would have a tree planted in Israel in honor of a special life event. A tree planted with love and attention could well outlive us, and quite often, give hundreds of years of enjoyment for generations to come. This is why I take pleasure in planting a tree to remind me of a special person or special time in my life. Over the years, I have planted many trees, each giving me great personal joy while providing interest to my home and garden.
A tree can make a touching gift or a powerful statement. I've been told, "it's the gift that keeps on giving." A dedication to a life or a celebration of a personal achievement makes the best reason, but for me, any reason will do.

My obsession truly began in 1997 when I bought my house and the property contained many old and diseased specimens. These majestic trees seemed to have a life force that I could sense and feel. Although I was reluctant and sad to lose these trees, I was soon involved in the happy adventure of choosing and planting their replacements, one for each tree removed (an excellent rule to adhere to.)

"By tending my garden, I make contact with the elements of life as I fine tune my skills and look to expand the ideas I have created. Gardens are metaphors for life and death."

Today there is no evidence of these old trees. My garden now boasts two white birches, one double trunk and one triple trunk, a flowering Japanese crabapple, and a Bradford pear among others. I chose these varieties for their flowers and varying heights. The crabapple has a low spreading habit and produces beautiful pink flowers in spring. The pear is ornamental, very tall and produces a bounty of white flowers before leafing out. The two birches have the eye-catching beauty of their magnificent white bark. Placing trees for height in low flower beds or as a focal point in the yard can give your garden architectural interest. Lighting each with a low halogen lighting system maximizes their beauty and impact in the evening.

In the spring of 2005, I planted, yet again, another tree picked and selected for its location. This time, I chose a semi dwaft Sekel pear. I dedicated this tree to my good friend and mentor, who passed away in April. I picked a special place to plant it where it would serve as a reminder of the many gifts he shared with me and others during his wonderful life. I watch this new addition grow through my kitchen window and find it rewarding to see the birds sit and enjoy a new place to relax in my garden. He would be delighted to know that Mother Nature and all her wildlife friends are enjoying his new tree. As it continues to grow and mature, I am constantly reminded how I, too, continue to grow from the bountiful memories and lessons he left behind.

Of the many reasons I could find to plant a tree, the best one of all is for the environment. Trees remove CO_2 from the air, produce oxygen and give birds a home. The planting of trees means improved water quality, less runoff and erosion. This allows more recharging of the ground water supply. In laboratory research, visual exposure to a setting with trees has been shown to produce significant recovery from stress within five minutes, as indicated by changes in blood pressure and muscle tension. Landscaping, especially with trees, can increase property values as much as 20 percent. The cultivation of trees is the cultivation of living things and a way of giving back to our communities.

When a tree is planted correctly, it will grow twice as fast and live at least twice as long as one that is incorrectly planted. For best results, plant new trees in the spring or fall. One thing to keep in mind in selecting your tree is that if you are able to carry it, you can plant it. Many garden centers and nurseries provide assistance in planting your new tree. If this is the case, make sure that you receive a warranty for this service. Most reputable nurseries will provide a one to two year warranty on your newly planted tree.

Besides you, your tree's best friend is mulch. Mulch insulates soil, retains moisture, and keeps the weeds out. It also prevents soil compaction, reduces lawnmower damage and adds an aesthetic touch to a yard or garden. It also serves as protection for the roots from extreme temperature fluctuations.

Once you have planted your new trees, caring for them is an important part of maintaining a healthy garden. Mature trees can become diseased if not treated regularly. Because it is difficult to know how your trees are doing, always hire a professional to care for, feed and provide pest control. While it is impossible to totally protect your trees and property from the elements of nature, there are some basic procedures that can help reduce the risk of damage. An arborist can inspect for defects and conditions that could predispose your trees to failure or future damage. They are also available to prune and shape your trees to grow to the size and proportions that appeal to you.

When selecting your tree, make sure you have the proper tree for the space and conditions you are choosing. Don't buy on impulse — no matter how beautiful it looks at the nursery. I see this mistake made over and over again. Do your homework! Research and ask lots of questions and enjoy the discovery process. Whether you plant a tree as a dedication or you're just looking to add interest and beauty to your home and garden, your relationship with your trees will intensify as the years go by. It will surely be a very rewarding experience. A tree for life…a life for a tree.

Fall is an excellent time to enjoy some hot chicken soup. It is good for the soul, good for the heart and even better for recovering from a cold. I'm always looking for comforting food that is easy to make. The healthy, nutritious and nostalgic dishes of our childhood may be just what our bodies and minds need on every level. I love this soup, and now find myself craving it. I hope you too can enjoy this simple but delicious chicken soup that is the heart of any feel-good recipe.

Grandma's Homemade Chicken & Escarole Soup

- 2-3 quarts of organic or homemade chicken stock
- 3 half chicken breasts (substitute in a full leg if you love dark meat)
- 1 head of escarole, cut into 2-3" pieces with a knife
- 1 cup of soup pasta such as tubettini or pastina
- 4 or 5 carrots, fine to medium diced
- 2 medium onions, finely diced
- 1 bay leaf
- 1 tablespoon of oregano
- ¼ cup of chopped parsley
- 3-5 tablespoons of olive oil
- Sea salt and freshly ground black pepper to taste
- 4 canned tomatoes, diced and patted dry
- 1 celery stalk, diced
- Water, as needed
- White wine or champagne vinegar
- Chunk of pecorino romano grated cheese

1. Chop celery, carrots and onions. Near the end of this process, begin heating olive oil in a large pan.

2. Sear chicken pieces until gently browned on all sides. Remove chicken from pan and set aside.

3. Add onions, celery and carrots to pan and sauté until onions are translucent. Transfer sautéed vegetables into soup pot. Next, add bay leaf, oregano and half of the parsley. Season with salt and pepper.

4. Add chicken stock and bring soup to boil, adding a splash of vinegar. Optional: Add tomatoes.

5. Return chicken to the soup pot. Allow soup to return to boil, and add in the escarole. Simmer or light boil for at least one hour. Be sure chicken is thoroughly cooked!

6. Remove chicken pieces from soup. Cut or tear them into small one inch pieces, discarding all bones and grisly skin. Return diced chicken to the soup pot.

7. Add remaining parsley, and season soup to taste. If you find the soup to be too thick, add water until desired consistency is reached.

8. Simmer or light boil one half hour. Ten minutes before serving, add pasta to the boiling soup.

9. Remove from heat. Add a splash of vinegar and a drizzle of olive oil.

10. Grate cheese over the top of the soup and serve.

Return cooled pot to the refrigerator for leftover lunches, appetizers or snacks. Can be frozen in plastic containers once cooled.

Cos-MAR-politan

- 3 parts vodka
- 1 part Cointreau® liqueur
- 1 part cranberry juice
- Juice of ½ to 1 fresh lime, depending on the size of the lime

After years of watching *Sex in the City*, where having a "Cosmo" was just about an everyday occurrence, I was inspired to create this sexy cocktail with a Mar twist. And if I could attract the same group of ladies around me, then my mission would be complete. With the help of my dear friend Geri, we perfected my version and it has become a signature drink in my home. Not just for fall, this recipe uses the best ingredients and is altogether a different cocktail from those you are likely to get in a bar. Try this one and you'll never order one out again.

1 Chill 2 martini glasses by filling them with ice and water. Put all ingredients over ice in a martini shaker.

2 Shake vigorously until a film of ice appears on the outside of the shaker.

3 Strain into the chilled martini glasses. Garnish with lime. Serves two.

Winter Tour

The soft arrival of new glistening snow creates unexpected beauty and serenity. All are asleep except the hardy evergreens with dramatically contrasting green and white. When I was a novice gardener, I paid no attention to the winter garden. Now that I am an experienced gardener, I have learned to create perspective, balance and harmony year round.

Each winter, I take the time to walk through my garden observing, pruning here and there, and picking up. If you go slowly, you feel as if in a dream. The Dwarf boxwood hedges seem dusted with powdered sugar, the new snow glimmering with silver lights. The outline of the resting Deciduous trees have a simple beauty. I notice dried leaves, grasses and colored berries everywhere. The birdhouses seem deserted, capped with snow. Amazing vistas open up with the leaves gone. I gaze across the winter landscape, and I am awed by the peace and timelessness of my winter garden. Returning to the hearth, I feel inspired as I look through my gardening books and magazines for fresh spring inspiration.

Painting shutters, trim, doors, etc.
a contrasting color such as high-gloss
black or dark green is a vibrant statement.
Having seen these high-gloss lacquered
doors everywhere in London, I wanted to
duplicate the effect. So, many years ago
I took the dramatic step of painting the
doors high-gloss black and added shiny
brass fixtures. In addition, I painted my
window boxes the same high-gloss black.
The result is a stunning contrast with the
dwarf boxwoods and the snow.

Pillars add grandness and can be an interesting architectural detail to any home. They should, however, be in scale with your house. Whenever possible, work them into your design. Climbing vines or roses can be trained around them. My two stone dogs rest contentedly, welcoming guests to the front door.

"It's winter. Amazingly, I still have a garden."

Intertwined Sombreuil and Eden Climber rose canes lie asleep on a soft arch trellis anchored by English boxwood holding the late afternoon snow. Texture and interest are present no matter what time of year it is.

Evergreen dwarf boxwoods are planted here in a serpentine pattern with larger anchor boxwoods behind to maintain a colorful green display of leaves that adds unusual interest. This simple architectural swirl reminds me of European gardens—a tiny piece of Versailles in my own backyard.

A 19th century stone urn filled with pine branches, holly branches, grasses, dogwood branches and other colorful leaves and berries give the urn an organic, alive feel in the winter garden. At Christmas, I put a glittery silver bow on it.

A little iron garden fence creates a focal point to what would normally be a dull and uninviting view. I pay close attention to small details — many people do notice these little touches. You too could not walk by this without taking notice. Note the antique rusted look.

Here one can see just how spectacular the English boxwood is when lined up and perfectly manicured. I often spend weekend afternoons pruning and fussing over them. The rewards are great, as you can see.

"Winter: my time for rest and renewal."

My Bacchus fountainhead frowns with a frozen stare. It is used here as a simple decorative wall hanging to alert garden wanderers that they are not alone.

Let us not forget about our little garden
friends. This wonderful birdhouse was
a gift that I cherish year after year.
No matter what the time of year, I can enjoy
the architectural sweetness of this cedar roof
birdhouse from indoors or out, as do the
sparrows and finches that live there.

The cement wicker-look planter holds a
spiral topiary created from an Alberta
spruce. I created this topiary by attaching a
ribbon at the top of the plant, wrapping the
ribbon around the plant, then cutting out
the branches in between the ribbon strands.
Voila, a topiary. To the right, a window box
explodes with winter branches.

Planters have increased meaning for me in the winter when they become a focal point
of color, interest and design. Here two lovely cement planters proudly display Alberta
spruces. Notice the high-gloss black garage door that adds contrast as a backdrop to the
lush evergreens and snow.

A teak garden bench is just as interesting a focal point in winter as in summer. A light snowfall defines the woven patterned back of this old bench.

This urn with a beautiful vine motif sits silently awaiting the call of spring.

This wooden trellis tuteur holds flowering vines in the spring and summer. The tuteur acts as an anchor point, giving contrasting height to the lower garden beds. In winter, it seems like a piece of sculpture with the swirling boxwoods below it.

"Respect the soil.
It's not dirt."

This little Pan statue seems frozen with the snow that covers him.
He is watching over the garden protecting his domain.

The intriguing bark of a birch tree creates interest and texture in the garden. In the blooming months, the white bark is a standout against the green landscape.

Dwarf boxwoods flow around the base of a crabapple tree. The backdrop of the trees' shadows on the fence reminds us that the sun can reach deep into this garden bed only in winter.

The view from my neighbor's yard. I get privacy, they get beauty. Although the Annabelle hydrangeas are dormant for the season, this garden bed still provides winter interest.

The front of the house and doorway are decorated in a classic and elegant style for the holidays. English boxwoods surround the front staircase.

"As I gaze through the window at the frost and snow, I feel the essence of the garden inside."

The garden studio stands starkly tall against the pale blue winter sky. This is a year round workplace where special projects are created.

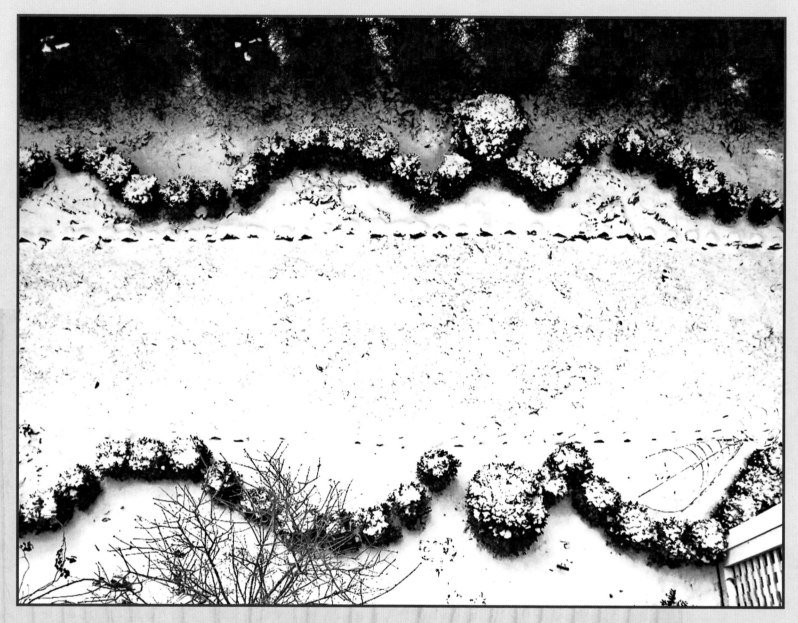

From my home office window, I stand and gaze at the dwarf boxwoods down below, swirling as if to seek the sun. The snow changes in brilliance as the sun moves across the garden beds.

A metal tuteur holds voluminous clematis in the spring and summer. The tuteur acts as an anchor point, giving height and color in the blooming season. In winter, it seems like a piece of sculpture with a swirl top that imitates the swirling boxwoods below it.

Winter Interest

Spring, summer and autumn are the seasons most enjoyed here in Connecticut. Although many love to ice skate, ski and snowboard, for gardeners like me, there is little or nothing to do in the garden. The vibrant exuberance of spring color, the lazy outdoor pleasure of summer, and the golden crispness of fall invites us into the garden to work, to entertain our friends, or to contemplate the beauty around us. In winter, the only thing we can do is look at our gardens from inside the house. That makes it essential to plan and create a garden that has lots of winter interest.

Winter starts pleasantly enough with the year-end holidays taking up most of our time and energy. But what are we to do after that? How can we continue to enjoy the garden after the blooming season? A garden needs to have the following things for winter interest: evergreens, focal points, architectural details and bird attractions.

Evergreens such as boxwood can be used throughout the garden in rows, as anchors, or as hedges. My favorite has always been the dwarf boxwood that I use as a diminutive hedge to outline the undulating curves of some of my beds. I can see them clearly from my dining room windows.

The variety of evergreens is overwhelming. They should be chosen for color and deer resistance and then planted in vignettes throughout your property. Combine them with other evergreen shrubs such as rhododendron, mountain laurel, azalea, winterberry, and holly to name a few. Leave the dried remnants of hydrangea, viburnum, sedum and ornamental grasses well into winter.

Creating focal points might involve a large stone or wood bench, a wall or a bridge, a cement or cast iron urn, a birdbath, concrete or lava balls, a statue, or well-placed boulders that fit in artistically among the evergreens and winter shrubs. I especially love the look of aged teak furniture on the patio or in the yard. Teak lasts forever and often takes on a beautifully weathered look. Use outdoor lighting to highlight each focal point. The lighting should be dim, casting a mysterious yet visible glow. Many gardeners forget about lighting, but it gets dark at 5:00 p.m. in the winter. All enjoyment is lost as the blackness of night descends, and you are unable to see beyond the reflection in the window.

The power of the allium flower, dried and sprayed gold. The perfect accent on this personally created holiday door wreath.

"In winter, the only thing we can do is look at our gardens
from inside the house. That makes it essential to plan
and create a garden that has lots of winter interest."

Specific examples of architectural details might be a stone patio, a driveway, an arbor, a pergola, a pathway, fencing, window boxes, or bricks to line the flowerbeds. For those who live in Connecticut or the adjoining states, remember that terra cotta and ceramic planters will crack, so take them in for the winter. The shape and layout of your flowerbeds define the architectural sense of your garden. I keep dwarf boxwoods in my window boxes surrounded by cascading annuals. In late autumn, I rip out the dead annuals and fill the boxes with dried hydrangea blossoms, holly and small evergreen branches for a hearty winter look.

Bird attractions require little explanation. Birdhouses, birdbaths and bird feeders will keep our fluttering friends in our backyards. I love to watch my resident cardinals with their red brilliance in sharp contrast to the white environment. I prefer birdseed in suet blocks because loose seed tend to get scattered about, causing weed problems in the spring. Be sure to tie down the suet block to avoid it being carried away by squirrels or crows, or in my case, a hungry Schnauzer.

A great place to visit for a more in-depth look at winter gardens is a nursery that specializes in winter plants and has a winter garden that you can walk through for ideas and inspiration. Buying trees, shrubs and evergreens is made easier by seeing the possible combinations in a model garden. However, the choices are so numerous that I recommend buying trees and plants that appeal to your sense of color and shape, taking into consideration hardiness, bloom time, sun and soil requirements. Add a few new items each spring with an eye towards winter appeal and each year your garden will increase in richness.

Local nurseries quite often offer free seminars on the art of garden design. Get on the mailing list of your favorite nurseries and check out their seminars, presentations and festivals. I like to keep current on the schedule at The New York Botanical Garden, where the variety and number of classes and seminars seems endless. After all, weekends in the winter can get dull, so why not take a course in gardening? The serenity and beauty of your winter garden will calm you, lighten your heart and warm your cold winter mood.

Since I have many trellises in my garden, I find myself frustrated when my climbing vines and roses die down and go dormant, leaving an unattractive bare trellis. It seems as if I were starting my garden all over again. So, for winter and the holiday season, I decorate my outdoor trellises with an abundance of evergreen clippings, dried magnolia leaves, Annabelle hydrangeas, bittersweet and holly all from my garden.

In early January right after the New Year, I'm ready to remove the holiday decorations. I recycle my holiday tree branches by cutting them into smaller pieces so I can add them to my wall trellises and even my planters. Nothing says "green" better than using green holiday clippings a second time around.

Should you not have any clippings of this type at home, just visit your local nursery and pick up whatever appeals to you. Do this in the month of December and watch how easy it is to get the cuttings of other people's holiday tree trimmings for free.

Once you have your branches and cuttings, it's very easy to slide the branches into trellis openings to secure them for the long winter months. This gives texture and color to what would normally be a bare and dreary sight. Come MARch, remove these branches before the resident vines or roses begin to show any activity.

John Barricelli of the SoNo Baking Company & Cafe in South Norwalk, CT was on the show and shared with me his apple tart recipe.

This recipe is perfectly simple (and great to do with kids) and simply the perfect apple tart! Winter is the perfect season to cook with apples.

The Perfect Apple Tart

- Puff pastry (usually available in the grocer's freezer section; defrost according to package directions)
- Four green apples, cored and sliced to a quarter inch
- Apple sauce
- A tin steel pan
- Confectioner's/powdered sugar

1 Preheat oven to 425 degrees.

2 Flour the work surface. Unroll the defrosted puff pastry and roll out flat to a quarter inch thickness. With a small knife, score about one inch from the edge all the way around. This will create a nice crispy border. Spread a thin layer of apple sauce on the pastry and lay the apples in rows, overlapping just a bit. Sprinkle with a healthy dose of confectioner's sugar using a sifter.

3 Bake for about 20-25 minutes or until golden brown. When it can move freely on the pan, it's done. Let cool for five minutes and serve immediately. Serves twelve.

As a former competitive skater, I'm no stranger to a good cup of hot chocolate. As a matter of fact, I believe it to be the drink of choice for any winter sport experience. While on vacation in Colorado recently, I had the craving for a good cup of hot chocolate after finishing an extremely rewarding day of snowboarding. When it arrived, I felt the inclination to give this classic drink a well deserved modern twist. Not having the ingredients on hand, I made a mental note to self that upon my return home, I would experiment and create a hot chocolate drink that I could call my own. That said, I now cannot image having a hot chocolate the traditional way unless, of course, you are under the age of 21.

So, this drink is dedicated to other aging athletes who, like me, are not in the same shape that we used to be but are still out there trying our best. This dreamy winter delight is the perfect après ski cocktail for those of us who are over the age of 21.

Mar's Dreamy Winter Delight

- 2 oz Brady's® Irish Cream liqueur
- Splash of Celtic Crossing® liqueur
- Canned whipped cream
- 1 serving hot chocolate mix
- Cinnamon, ground or stick
- Fresh chocolate shavings to garnish

1 Warm a mug by pouring boiling water into it and letting it sit for a minute or two. Pour the two liqueurs into the warm mug. Add prepared hot chocolate. If you like your chocolate really hot, warm the liqueur first but be careful not to boil it.

2 Garnish with whipped cream. Add cinnamon. I prefer to place a cinnamon stick through the whipped cream. As a bonus, top with chocolate shavings. Now you're ready to relax by a fire and enjoy.

Spring Tour

Every year as I begin to anticipate spring during the long winter days, I often awake with a burst of energy propelling me to get to work in the garden. Vivid memories come from those early March days when I plant seeds in my garden studio. My preparation is meticulous. I typically spend the winter months deciding what changes to make and what new plants will be added to my ever-growing gardens. Spring in Westport can be decidedly chilly in March and even April, with a balmy seventy degree day followed by a frigid windy day the next, causing me to worry about my new plantings. My snow drops and crocuses may have been out for a while, but it's not until the first yellow daffodil opens that I know the season has truly turned to spring. Spring is about new beginnings. My garden reminds me of that each and every year. As I look around my gardens, I focus on the beauty and new life that continues to inspire me personally.

My garden is filled with purple and white alliums that create height and interest in the garden. Here is the beginning as they break through and begin their amazing display.

When the irises begin to bloom, I know the garden will soon be filled with beauty and intensity. An endless amount of flowers will be displayed as guests are welcomed to the back garden bed.

The crabapple tree is filled with delicate white and pink flowers bursting from every branch. Each year, a spectacular display announces that spring has finally arrived. This tree was planted in honor of a dear friend that has passed away. It not only serves as a reminder, but each year it's as if he speaks to me through the power of nature.

Daffodils are displayed within a boxwood hedge. The contrast of color adds interest to the border. I clump the bulbs together in groups of eight to twelve for maximum visual impact.

"Why pay for therapy when the garden needs tending?"

This classic, pink rhododendron was on the property prior to my home being built in 1996. While I respect her tenure, she is not in the best place in the garden. I trimmed this old lady rhododendron back and incorporated her into my new garden design. Although she weeps in the cold days of winter warning me of the chill in the air, come spring her blossoms are welcoming and filled with new life.

For many of us, wisteria can be difficult to re-bloom. I discovered years ago that Amethyst Falls continues to bloom on new growth several times within the season. Although the flowers are not as spectacular as the classic wisteria we all love, Amethyst Falls has, nevertheless, won my heart. This wisteria is guaranteed to provide you with blooms year after year.

Almost lost

several year

to maintain

Here is another example of something original in the garden planted prior to my arrival. This white dogwood is so filled with flowers in the early spring that it captures the neighbors' attention from across the street. Almost lost due to an ice storm that split its trunk several years ago, I now regularly trim its branches to maintain its perfect shape. Notice the burning bush below that adds contrast to the dogwood above.

Having clematis in the garden is a fantastic way to start your spring. With over twenty varieties throughout my garden, I enjoy each and every one. Here, one begins to see what is to become a marvelous display of color.

Myrtle is commonly available in the garden center. However, should you happen to find the white variety, you're in for a real treat. White myrtle is not as available as the purple and sells out rather quickly. Using white myrtle as the ground cover of choice, I transformed my side garden into something quite unique, something one doesn't see everyday.

Small Snowflake Candytuft is spreading over the bricks onto the grass. This delicate but sweet crawler comes back each and every year, better than the last.

"No need to wait for spring when you have MARch."

The Eden Climber was the first rose I planted in my garden eight years ago. Knowing that I wanted a fragrant climber, I searched David Austin's Handbook of Roses to select the perfect rose for my arbor. I picked the Eden Rose for its rounded, deeply cupped full flowers of creamy white with pink-edged petals. This special rose is strikingly beautiful and gorgeous for clipping.

After all the flowering trees have finished blooming in the early spring, the Styrax Japonica starts its magic. Blooming in June, it provides an unexpected splash in the garden. Its bell flower is exceptionally fragrant and is incredibly interesting in the garden even after the flowers are gone.

The Endless Summer hydrangea is a new addition to my always expanding garden. While containers are typically for annuals, I've placed this perennial in a terra cotta container for the season and will transplant it into the side garden come fall. A "bang for the buck" I call this, as I get lots of mileage from this one plant.

Perfect harmony is created as peonies and irises unite in the garden. My garden is filled with interesting and surprising combinations. One never knows what one might discover at Rosebrook Gardens.

This pink Evithree welcomes visitors to the herb garden.

This delicate, white allium was purposely planted
close to the walkways because of its extended
blooming time and for height. In late spring, I remove
them intact and dry them. Then, come winter,
I spray them with gold or silver paint and add them
to holiday wreaths for a dramatic touch of spring.

Over twenty-two white and pale pink peonies cover the two-section picket fence,
creating a breathtaking display of color. This announces that spring has arrived,
is in full swing, and entices you to take a peek over the fence to discover more.
A bold, dark purple clematis was chosen as a contrast to this incredible display.

My Wisteria

This is my second attempt at getting my wisteria to produce flowers. I have two different varieties that rise up and crown the top of my pergola. One wisteria is a special variety called Amethyst Falls. It is fast growing, smaller and less invasive than Asian wisterias. Amethyst Falls flowers sporadically spring through summer. It blooms on current year's growth. This is an excellent addition to your garden. Although the flowers are not as abundant as regular single flowering varieties, it's guaranteed to flower. If you choose to go with the more traditional wisteria, here's a tip; buy a more mature plant from the nursery with blooms already on it. This way, you can be fairly certain that your wisteria will, in fact, bloom.

The second wisteria on my pergola has bloomed this year with endless amounts of flowers. Each year, I prune it throughout the summer to maintain its direction and shape. I also remove all of the little straggling tendrils from the main stem. Every garden expert seems to have a different theory about how to make wisteria bloom. In addition to maintenance pruning, I also prune heavily after the blooming season.

Feed your wisteria with super phosphate in early spring. That will encourage blooms. Of course, full sun is essential. Root pruning can help too. Make cuts in the roots with a shovel 2 to 3 feet away from the plants. Do this late spring or early summer after bloom time.

Wisteria offers so much to your garden, but requires annual attention. Whether you select the classic purple or the uncommon white flowering wisteria, this is one vine worth owning. Over a pergola, there is nothing more romantic or beautiful in the garden.

Pasta is one of my favorite foods and, though many of my friends refuse to eat it, I simply refuse to give it up. Pasta should always be cooked "al dente," which means "to the bite." Properly cooked pasta is firm and slightly chewy, but never mushy.

Use only pasta made from durum semolina. This type of wheat is hard (as opposed to soft), will remain firm if not overcooked and has more fiber. I only use imported Italian brands of pasta because I have found that they taste better. You can find organic, whole grain pasta in better supermarkets and specialty stores. It's worth it.

This is a version of the classic dish "Spaghetti con aglio et olio" which means spaghetti with garlic and oil. I hope you like it as much as I do.

Pasta with Fresh Herbs

- 6 quarts of water
- 2 tbsp kosher salt
- 1 lb. organic whole wheat spaghetti
- 4 or 5 garlic cloves, peeled and cut into little sticks
- ¼ cup fresh basil, chopped
- ¼ cup fresh parsley, chopped
- 2 tbsp fresh thyme, chopped
- 2 tbsp fresh rosemary, chopped
- ¾ cup extra virgin olive oil
- ¼ tsp red pepper flakes
- 1 cup freshly grated parmesan cheese
- 2 tsp grey salt (or to taste)
- ½ tsp fresh black pepper (or to taste)

1 Sauté the garlic in ¼ cup of the olive oil until lightly browned and crispy. Move the pan from the heat. Remove the garlic to a small dish and add the remaining ½ cup of oil to the pan so it will infuse with the garlic flavor. Add the red pepper flakes to the oil.

2 Bring the water to a rolling boil in a large pot. Add the kosher salt. While the water is coming to a boil, chop the herbs and grate the cheese.

3 Drop pasta in the water gently. DO NOT break the spaghetti in half. Cook two minutes less than the package directions. Use a timer and when it goes off, start checking the pasta to make sure it does not overcook. When the pasta is just tender, drain in a colander and transfer to a large, shallow bowl. Add the olive oil, herbs, cheese, garlic, salt and pepper to taste. Toss gently.

Thank You

Laura Baker from Picket's for being a wonderful resource for my home and garden.

Eric Barber from Connecticut Arborists for his amazing talent in maintaining and nurturing my trees.

Michael Bensey from Straight Line Landscaping for ten years of patience with my micromanaging and going above and beyond.

Chris Brown from Teed & Brown for giving me a lush, carpet-like lawn year after year.

Steve Cowell for taking me on as a client, acknowledging my prolificity, and motivating me to write more books.

Marco Soto from Dobson Irrigation for your professionalism and devotion to my garden.

HB&T for being the most amazing organization. I am motivated to excel simply by being a part of this team.

Randy Herbertson and Seesaw for their endless support and dedication to this book.

Ross Mastrorocco from Enviro Designs for accepting my unconventional patio design and executing it to perfection with his talented team.

Greenfield Hill Nursery and Oliver's Nursery for their personalized service and great selection.

My neighbors for their acceptance and generosity of spirit.

The Town of Westport, CT and the many people and charities that have helped me grow and develop both personally and professionally.

Stephen Carta for appreciating my talents and creativity and allowing me to use them.

The Dodd Family: Lori, Jason, Sophie & Reilly for always being there for me and for becoming my extended family.

J.C for being a wonderful brother when I needed you most.

Tom Lialios: words cannot express the depth of my gratitude for believing in me.

Barbara Mathias for being the best friend and neighbor a person could have. I'll forever be your Marsley!

Patricia Rodriguez for your wonderful supportive friendship that has lasted beyond our banking relationship.

Geri Zatcoff for holding my hand and for keeping her promise to Edward.